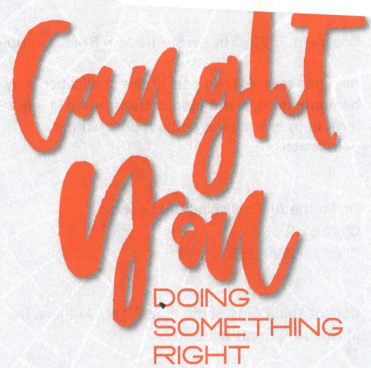

Caught You
DOING SOMETHING RIGHT

DR. MATTIE JO & BRENT JOHNSON

UALLo.w.e.d Publishing
Chicago, IL

Copyright 2022 © by Dr. Mattie Jo & Brent Johnson

All rights reserved. No part of this publication may be reproduced, distributed or transmitted in any form or by any means, without prior written permission.

Dr. Mattie Jo/Publishing UALLo.w.e.d
Chicago, IL
www.uallowed.com

Caught You! Doing Something Right/ Authors. Dr. Mattie Jo & Brent Johnson
1st ed.
ISBN 978-0-9990125-0-5

Cover Design:
Rachael Turner, Rosemint Media

DEDICATION

This book is dedicated to those who LOVE with everything in them. We want you to REMEMBER that if you want it, you can definitely have it. Your relationship will not, should not, can not look like ANYONE else's because there is NO ONE like you or your mate. It is the uniqueness of your relationship that will help you survive.

When it seems like you have tried it all TRY AGAIN.
To love and be loved is one of the greatest things you can experience on earth.

Contents

INTRODUCTION
5

MATTIE & BRENT'S RELATIONSHIP
6

ABOUT THE EXPERIMENT
14

QUIZ
18

RELATIONSHIP PLAN
29

THE *Caught You* CHALLENGE
39

INTRODUCTION

So many times, in life when we hear the word <u>*CAUGHT*</u>; especially when it comes to relationships, we automatically think the worst. Have you ever wondered why that is? Is it that over the years when we hear the stories of people getting caught up in relationships there is a negative connotation associated with it?

Hopefully after reading our book, you will have a new outlook on catching your mate doing something. Our 31-day journey of catching each other doing something right will help you love, cherish, and bring one another closer. So, prepare yourself to catch your mate doing something RIGHT.

Brent & Mattie's Relationship

BIO OF MATTIE AND BRENT'S RELATIONSHIP
from their different perspectives

HOW MATTIE AND BRENT MET?
Mattie's Recollection

It was Spring of 2007. I had a recent break-up with a guy whom I just knew without a doubt was the ONE. He seemed to be ideal. I felt like yessss this was the relationship I was dreaming of. I also felt like the breakup was just me and the guy needing a breather and him telling me it was not his job to make sure my feet were sandal ready was just a silly reason among others to not get back together. Right? However, at that time I was living in Georgia, and did not know many people so of course I called up a friend who was tech savvy and asked her to upgrade my MYSPACE page. LISTENNNN!!!!! Do not laugh at me. Anyway! The purpose of the upgraded page was to find some guys to have some fun for the holiday weekend. Although I was going through a breakup, I knew it was going to be on and popping because I had five dates lined up from all my social media pages. My best friend and I was going on some free dates.

Thank you, MYSPACE. SOOO one of those free dates was with my now husband. He slipped in my inbox well it is called DMs now with "hey cutie." I'm like Heeeeeeeyyyyy.... because he was kind of cute you know. We began to write back and forth, and I realized he had an amazing personality we really hit it off until I began to ask the big questions; *Do you have any children?* His response was yes, and I was like ok. I have 1 son; *how many you have?* He responds six. SIX CHILDREN!!!!! *Like how? Like why?* So many questions swirled through my mind and the ultimate question that surely let me know he was not the one for me was, *how many baby mamas?* His response was three at the time (I save the last one for another time). My response after that was; *Oh, hell naw! God gone bless you with somebody that's going to love you and all those babies.* He then began to tell me how if a woman could not accept ALL his children, then she could basically kick rocks. This man loved those babies, and they were his priority.

Shhhhh for me that was kind of attractive. Heeeeyyyyy boo! This was sexy to me especially being a single mother who had a child by a guy who wouldn't own up to the responsibility of his child. Although, fathering his children was attractive; it was a major red flag that he fathered them with multiple women. Moving forward we continued to talk which led to us deciding to meet on Memorial Day. Although he had a great personality, I did not expect much to come of us meeting but some laughs and jokes. Now when I saw him in person my thought was well maybe we can have a little fun. My friend Penny was with me, and she stated, "Brent was the one." Penny went on to ask if I saw the bible on his tv. Now for me that was not a sign of him being no better than anyone else; I stated his bible was just for decorations in a joking matter.

Brent's Recollection

We met with a simple "Hey Cutie" on MySpace. Lol. We both had just recently came out of a relationship and was just online looking to meet someone to kick it with. The first time we met I realized she was prettier and sexier than her profile pic. She came over with her friend and we talked and kicked it for a little while. She had a date with another guy set up later that day, so she couldn't stay as long. She had my attention from the time she walked through the door, I texted her the WHOLE time she was on her other date, and she must have liked it because she was texting back.

After dating for a while, we eventually met each other kids (my 6 and her 1), I made it known that the person who I married would have to accept my me and my kids. Her response was "Good Luck, that's too many for me". As the year went by, we continue dating and enjoying each other company and started to plan our wedding which was postponed because I ended up dating and moving in with someone else which is when we found out Mattie was pregnant with my youngest daughter Journey. Due to my indiscretions, she decided not to let me in the delivery room while my daughter was being born until and friend convinced her otherwise. (Stubborn Azz lol).

I remember signing the birth certificate and the nurse asked what my address was, and I provided her with my new address which was with the young lady I was dating. Mattie waited to the nurse left to say "Oh so you are giving the wrong address now" she wasn't aware the young lady and I had moved in together. Once that relationship did not work out, I began to pursue Mattie again and eventually that led to us replanning our wedding. I had to plan everything because Mattie didn't really believe that I had changed. She didn't care to have a wedding, but I felt she deserved one and I wanted her to have one.

HOW LONG WE'VE BEEN TOGETHER?

Mattie's Recollection

Brent and I met the Summer of 2007. Our relationship was kind of rocky. We became pregnant 3 months after knowing one another. We were set to get married in November of that same year however, Brent was in another relationship that I clearly was not aware of so that wedding was called off. After much back and forth, ins and outs during the next year and half Brent decided to ask me to marry him. This was not an easy decision however I wanted my daughter to grow up with her father. So here we are 12 years later writing a book together. We will be going into our teen age years of marriage this year.

Brent's Recollection

Us being from two different states was a challenge on where to have the wedding but we decided to have it in Atlanta my place of birth. Marriage was the BEST decision I ever made in my life. This woman has showed me how to live, travel, and become a better man, father, coach, mentor and person all around. I could never imagine my life today without her.

We've been together 2 years on and off, married 12 so a total of 14 years. These years have had their challenges of ups & downs but the desire to fight through has been the key to maintaining our marriage. The day I saw her walking down the aisle in her wedding dress was the highest level of happiness for me. I couldn't stop crying from the beginning to the end of the wedding, even while exchanging vows one another children. After several obstacles we are still married and going strong. The realization that anything worth having is worth fighting for has been one of my motivations. We are one another balance, she is strong where I need improving and vice versa.

MATTIE'S INSIGHT ON BRENT
What Made Mattie Say Yes

I spoke a little of the ups and downs of our relationship however, in all honesty what made me say yes to Brent was the simple fact he was a great father. Every summer while living in Georgia I sent my son back to Chicago to visit his and my godmother Sandra. So, I was able to have maybe too much fun. However, when my son who was six years old at the time came back home, he met Brent and ALL THOSE KIDS and jumped on his lap looked at me and smiled and started calling him Dad immediately. Ummmmm, how could I not want to keep this man. Now I know for many this was not a reason to marry and maybe you are right however, this was one of the only reasons at the time; that I wanted to marry. I wanted my son to have a male in the home. Now of course there were other qualities that made me want to hold on to this guy too like; he was a hard worker. He had never called off his job in seven years. I was such a bad influence. I told him Well you sick today call off so we can go out. I loved his work ethic. I knew I was a hard worker but if anything was to happen where I could not work my son and I would be taken care of.

What Mattie Love's About Brent

Brent has never met a stranger. I love how giving he is to any and everyone. To many in relationships this can be a problem and honestly many times it has brought forth some challenges with us. However, it has been better than bad. I love his heart for others

What Has been the Challenge for Mattie with Brent?

Brent is less of a talker and will just do. However, I need the communication. I need to know your understanding what I'm saying and give me some feedback to what is being communicated.

BRENT'S INSIGHT ON MATTIE
What Made Brent Say Yes

What made me say yes was the way she loved me and all the extra that came with me. She saw me at my worst and still decided to love me. Originally, she was like "I'll Pass" but my charms and handsomeness won her over.

What Brent Loves About Mattie

Mattie's greatness is her drive to make sure our family is LIVING and not just existing. I've watched her excel and conquer any tasks she takes on. Watching her tackle all the drama around obtaining her Doctorate Degree was the most inspiring.

What Has been the Challenge for Brent with Mattie?

Mattie lack of patience at times drives me crazy. Often, I must remind her that her level of thinking & processing is above the average person therefore she can't get frustrated, and she need to be more patient.

The Experiment

THE EXPERIMENT

Why?

Full transparency of how why this book came about. I was growing weary in our relationship and got to the point of wanting to call it quits. I felt like the communication would never get better it would just be me being blunt about how I felt and him getting upset about what I said and then telling me what he didn't like suddenly. Remember this is post Covid and mid pandemic. We both were probably just sick of one another.

So, while going on about my day the still small voice spoke to me and said for the next month ask Brent to join you in catching each other doing something right. Now LISSSSSTEN this still small voice came after I had already decided I was done and just didn't want this anymore; however, I try my best to obey that small voice because it leads and guides me in ALL TRUTH whether I want to hear it or not. One thing I love about Brent is he knows my still small voice be on point, so he usually listens to it too. In August of 2021 we decided to go on a mission to catch one another doing something right verses what we felt was wrong.

Why was this needed? For some reason it is always easy to find fault in others because often we see our problems through our own lens. The emotions make it more difficult to be objective and make logical decisions. What was revealed to me was that often time it's easy to find flaws because in some form of fashion we want to feel validated. What I'm learning in this journey of marriage is when I am wrong admit it and when I'm right which is most of the time, to be quiet.

The experiment of catching my husband doing something right was difficult; not because he wasn't doing things right but because I had to come to the realization that I was taking many things he had done for granted. Small actions are a powerful tool that adds love and life to the marriage. This experiment was a small road we travelled to achieve a better marriage. Let this experiment help you develop a culture of gratitude which help us to easily catch our mate doing something right. The experiment is not a process to change someone else but to discover spoken and unspoken language and touches that are meaningful while becoming a partner of gratitude.

We would love to challenge you to CATCH YOUR SPOUSE (significant other, partner) doing something right. You may ask the question what does catching my spouse doing something right do? Let me share three reasons how catching your spouse doing something right can help your relationship.

1. RID the relationship of a toxic culture.

> Finding the value in my husband help to rid our relationship of toxic thinking that society often place on us. I began to not judge the way he washed our clothes and became thankful that he wasn't a husband that felt like that wasn't a role for his gender. I rid the relationship of toxic culture by intentionally becoming more vulnerable with him although I have a more dominate nature. Toxic culture especially for black, educated, strong woman many times make women feel that we must remain strong even with our spouse. I rid the relationship of a toxic culture by taking off my superwoman cape once I entered our home.

2. Help to find out root issues and deal with past wounds.

While catching my husband doing things right; him working in his passion was something often, I loved and hated. However, when questioning him about why he was so dedicated to kids outside of the 10 we have biologically allowed us to get to the root issue of not having a parent at his games or track meets which left a sore spot for him. He made a vow to always be there to support those in his life.

3. Help you embrace the call to greatness.

Often when counseling married couples, I explain my understanding of my marriage being more about ministry than one another. Our marriage has assisted hundreds if not thousands of youths in the city of Chicago. We founded an organization called Back 2 the Basics that assisted youth in starting or refreshing their paths that value empathy, compassion, tolerance, trust and love for themselves as well as their neighbor. These things will help them in the long run to keep doing their absolute best. Going back to the basics is just a return to a simpler way of doing things. So, in embracing our call to greatness we began to understand it was all in the simplicity of loving one another minute by minute, hour by hour, day by day, month by month, year by year. When we stick to the basics, we learn to be ok even in our mess ups.

Quiz

QUIZ: ARE YOU A GRATITUDE PARTNER?

Answer Yes or No

1. Do you consistently think of ideas to please your partner?
2. Do you usually care about the quality of time and less about the quantity of time with your partner?
3. Do you feel successful in the relationship, but aren't sure if you can be successful on your own?
4. Do you know your relationship is destined for great things but feel like it's taking too long to manifest?
5. Does being in a relationship feel constricting, and you don't want to answer to your mate?
6. Have you tried communication techniques that did not work but you still have the passion to try new ones?
7. Does the idea of being in a relationship with one person for the rest of your life scare you?
8. Do you feel like success in the relationship is in your power, but you don't want to rely on your mate?
9. Have you always wanted to be in control of your own time and experiences, but right now you feel like you are just trying to get by?
10. Do you have the idea of waiting until something else happen to enjoy your life?

QUIZ: ARE YOU A GRATITUDE PARTNER?

Answer Yes or No

11. Do you want to do more in your relationship, but your mate do not?

12. Do you want to give more in the relationship but feel unable to right now?

13. Are you able to plan with your partner?

14. Do you look at other successful relationships and think, "What made them successful? will we ever make it?

15. Do you wish to extend your family?

16. Do you want to become a better partner through personal growth, even if it's difficult?

17. Have you ever lost sleep due to excitement about the possibilities of your relationship?

18. Are you willing to put in the work that matter, or just get by?

If you answered yes to at least half of the questions, you are most likely on your way to being partner of gratitude. You want to forge a path with your partner full of freedom quality and love. Most importantly you want your relationship build something that you both truly enjoy. You are already successful in many areas in your relationship, even if you don't feel like it. (You have high expectations!)

Even if you said no to more than half of these, keep reading. Maybe you haven't thought about what you fully want out of the relationship, but you will soon discover why becoming a partner of gratitude is your best bet to a beautiful relationship. Don't worry if you don't feel like you can get past issues within the relationship. Many people who continued their relationships after hard times felt the same way.

SIGNIFICANT FINDINGS AND REACTIONS TO THE EXPERIMENT
Believing in What You Have

Your choices in life have brought you to where you are in life and the relationship you are in. We often do not admit how much control our choices have but they determine what you both will accomplish together. The freedom you both receive in the relationship is key to moving forward. You both have the power to change your relationship outcome and it all begins with your choices to love one another for the day that is present. You both want your relationship to work for you not against you. We know many times we learned the hard way. On this journey we will figure out what you both value, how much trust you really have, how to rid toxic thinking, and how to start devoting time to one another.

Finding what you value

Think of the last 5 things you've done for or with your spouse. Write them down (including things like running bath water, foot rub, going on a date, or fixing their plate):

1._____

2._____

3._____

4._____

5._____

After you had done these things, how did you feel? Think about that feeling. Was there love, guilt, or passion contributing to your decision to do for your partner. Was it done as a chore? Mark an X next to what you were really happy about. Look at those with the X next to them and let this give you an idea of what you value in your relationship.

SUMMARY OF BELIEVING IN WHAT YOU HAVE

Rule #1 – Get Honest

We say get honest because it refers to some sort of CHANGE or process.

Rule #2 – Be Conscious of the value of the relationship

Principle 1: Enjoy many small pleasures instead of a few big ones (limited to holidays)
Principle 2: Think of your mate instead of just yourself
Principle 3: Have experiences instead of things in the relationship

Rule #3 – Intentions don't count

Rule #4 – Examine your choices

WEEKLY VALUE FORM

Values	Su	M	T	W	T	F	Sa
Companionship							
Respect							
Empathy							
Vulnerability							
Accountability							
Commitment							
Trust							
Communication							

These are just examples of values that couples share within their relationship and are generally the happiest and healthiest. If these are not your core values, feel free to swap them out. This is a weekly accountability reminder for the month you're catching your spouse doing something RIGHT.

FEARS, EXCUSES, AND ISSUES OF CONFIDENCE IN THE RELATIONSHIP

One of the fears one may have in a relationship is that this may not last, or we make up excuses why we shouldn't be vulnerable and lack confidence in relationships because we have idols in our head that no one can measure up to. It is time to tare down those idols. It is easy to compare our thoughts of fear, struggle, and lack of confidence to idol images of social media, Hollywood, or couples we deem successful. Let's put all relationships on a level playing field by identifying our strengths and fears by taking action to push our self and our partner out of your daily comfort zone.

Feedback With Tough Love

Ask a trusted couple, individual friends, or even a mate to give you honest and constructive criticism about your interactions with your mate and love habits. This may be painful to hear, but it will be one of the fastest ways to get you to notice them.

1—does not display

2—only occasionally display

3—usually displays

4—always displays

5—goes above and beyond to display

INTERACTIONS WITH YOUR MATE/ LOVE HABITS

Appears to be happy when with your mate

1   2   3   4   5

Dependability

1   2   3   4   5

Commitment to your partner

1   2   3   4   5

Judgemental

1   2   3   4   5

Protective

1   2   3   4   5

Shows initiative

1   2   3   4   5

Fraternizing

1   2   3   4   5

Decision making

1   2   3   4   5

Prioritize the relationship

1   2   3   4   5

Credibility

1   2   3   4   5

Take some time and see what those closest to you have to say about what you are displaying to them. After you have taken it all in spend time focusing on areas to improve. My husband and I love this song by H.E.R called "Focus". The song writer describes how she don't want to give up on the relationship, but she wants her mate to get up because lately she has been a little fed up and wishes that her mate would just focus on her. Is everything on your plate moving your relationship forward. What are you focusing on? Bite off small chunks. Give yourself daily goals then move on to a weekly, or monthly goal. More than anything just FOCUS.

Relationships are truly an investment, and you must ask yourself how much time which we know is money are really investing. Make a list and write down all the things you would like to be able to do in your relationship. Then research it to see how to get the results you want.

How much time do I really have to invest?

List of things you would like to do in your relationship.

Once you create your list just act for today not the entire relationship. We learned to love one another enough for today.

List your single action:

_____

FEARS WITHIN THE RELATIONSHIP

What truly scares you? Write it down. You don't have to speak of it to anyone, but it needs to be brought to light. Being able to pinpoint what scares you allows you to deal with it and usually its false evidence appearing real meaning it's all in our imagination. Now don't get me wrong because our imagination can be powerful. Therefore, we will shine light on our fear to help us move beyond them.

What scares you when it comes to relationships? When it comes to being with me?

Again, let's choose an action to commit to the next time you become scared within our relationship.

- Acknowledge my vulnerability with a situation we are having
- Feel my feelings
- Understand some things will take time with time
- Choose to believe my partner feels I'm worthy to be with them
- Explain a trigger point
- Encourage openness on both ends
- Put things in perspective

Relationship Plan

RELATIONSHIP PLAN

Let's write a relationship plan, figuring out what ideal days would look like, and even figuring out the strengths and weaknesses of the relationship with a SWOT analysis.

1. Grab a sheet of paper.
2. Draw a line in the middle.
3. Write your age at the far left
4. Place an idea in each section

AGE	IDEA
_44_	<u>Take stepping class</u>
___	_____
___	_____
___	_____
___	_____
___	_____
___	_____
___	_____
___	_____

LET'S PLAN THE IDEAL DATE

Write out your ideal date. We want to be as detailed as possible. This will always be a go to (cheat sheet) until desires change.

- _____
_____
- _____
_____
- _____
_____
- _____
_____
- _____
_____
- _____
_____
- _____
_____
- _____
_____
- _____
_____

What do you consider to be the ideal life?

- _____
  _____
- _____
  _____
- _____
  _____
- _____
  _____
- _____
  _____
- _____
  _____
- _____
  _____
- _____
  _____
- _____
  _____

Now let's create a relationship SWOT analysis from some of the ideas you all came up with. We will delve into what each of us feel is ideal so we can see a clear picture of what we are up against. What do we mean? A lot of the things we mentioned as ideal are idols we have in our head that we never uttered to our spouse so, inside our relationship we have been in competition with these unspoken idols.

A relationship SWOT analysis (strengths, weaknesses, opportunities, threats) is a tool to really determine what the relationship looks like. This will give you a better picture of what you are dealing with.

List 5 things you both do well: *Strengths within the relationship* (Ex. We both are great communicators)

_____

_____

_____

_____

_____

List 5 things you feel your relationship need.
Weaknesses within the relationship
(Ex. Refuses to deal with anger issues)

_____

_____

_____

_____

_____

_____

_____

_____

_____

_____

List 5 opportunities each of you would like to try to enhance the relationship.
(Ex. Trying therapy as a couple)

_____

_____

_____

_____

_____

_____

_____

_____

_____

_____

List 5 threats that have come up against your relationship.
(Ex. Outside family members)

_____

_____

_____

_____

_____

Take these list and ideas and talk to one another to come up with a plan for your relationship. Begin to solve the problems with small steps. Remember this is a process. Often, we want good to happen in the relationship until it requires us to become better. List one item that you both want to work on today.

YOUR RELATIONSHIP HAS A SERIES OF SMALL WINS

We all love it when everything seems to be great and full of success. It can range from that first kiss to finally saying "I Do." It can even be deciding that you need more time to work on yourself before taking the first action toward another relationship. It all adds up to where you are now.

Creating A Vision

Step 1: The future is creating a vision of who you want to be in your relationship Think about 5 or even 10 years in the future.

Who are you in your vision? Are you confident and traveling the world? Is this how you act now? Write a list of characteristics that you want to describe you in the future.

_____   _____

_____   _____

_____   _____

_____   _____

If this is difficult ask your mate or someone who has the characteristics you want to manifest. Write those down.

Step 2: The future of your relationship

Where is the relationship going?
_____
_____
_____
_____

Will you both be in love?
_____
_____
_____
_____

What will be the legacy of your family?
_____
_____
_____
_____

VISION: CRYSTAL CLEAR

Your vision for yourself and your partner will help to push you both into covenant- solemn agreement.

The goal is to declare what you want your relationship to look like now and in the future. The covenant takes actions.

1. Commit to catching your partner doing something right for the next month.

2. Create a scheduled reminder to SEE your mate.
    - **S**- single out efforts and think on it
    - **E**- exercise restraint with judgments
    - **E**- envision the best possible future

For my husband and I to catch each other doing something right we had to be intentional in seeing one another. We both noticed more things about one another that we may have not noticed prior to the experiment. What was so interesting to me was the fact that everything my husband saw; were things I felt he had taken for granted. When I read the things, my husband caught me doing right; tears filled my eyes because he didn't just notice actual things, I was doing but he also jotted down my effort in trying to do things that he knew was rather difficult for me.

This experiment heightened our gratitude for one another, and we hope this help to give you and your mate, partner, significant other, or spouse the boost you need to begin or start over in rekindling your love for one another.

The Caught You Doing Something Right Challenge

Day 1

TODAY GIVE A COMPLIMENT ON SOMETHING OTHER THAN YOUR PARTNER PHYSICAL APPEARANCE

Compliments help us communicate appreciation, shows value and expresses approval. A compliment has the power to improve your partner day.

What was your partner's reaction from the compliment?

_____
_____
_____
_____
_____
_____
_____

How do you feel after giving the compliment and getting the reaction?

_____
_____
_____
_____
_____
_____
_____
_____

Day 2

WRITE A SIMPLE NOTE ACKNOWLEDGING YOUR MATE CONTRIBUTION TO THE RELATIONSHIP

Acknowledgement makes others feel motivated and positive. This makes it more likely for them to repeat this behavior in the future. Acknowledgement is linked to higher fulfillment.

_____

_____

_____

_____

_____

_____

_____

_____

_____

_____

_____

Day 3

TODAY DO SOMETHING THAT MAKES YOUR PARTNER SMILE.

The brain releases tiny molecules called neuropeptides to help fight off stress.

Make your partner stress free today.

😃

Day 4

TODAY TAKE TIME TO L.I.S.T.E.N TO YOUR SPOUSE!

Listening to your spouse help you to understand and feel closer and more connected to your partner.

L- Learn something new
I- Ignore distractions while conversating
S- Stick to the issue they are speaking of
T- Take necessary action after the talk
E- Empathize
N- Nonverbal cues show that you

_____

_____

_____

_____

_____

_____

_____

_____

_____

Day 5

SURPRISE YOUR SPOUSE WITH SOMETHING THEY BEEN ASKING FOR.

Surprises in the relationship brings in excitement as well experiences. Slip out of the pattern of not making effort in the relationship.

Shift your relationship to a new level!

_____
_____
_____
_____
_____
_____
_____
_____
_____
_____
_____

Day 6

CREATE A SEXY WISH LIST.

Let's create a risqué list of all the things you'd like for your partner to do to or for you sexually. When and where can be your secret...

1. _____
2. _____
3. _____
4. _____
5. _____
6. _____

I know you can fill this whole page, however, are you comfortable talking about sex with your partner. Have you ever had a real down to earth conversation about your likes or dislikes in the bedroom?

Ask:

**What do I do in the bedroom that you love?
Is there anything I do in the bedroom that you dislike?**

_____

How often would you like to have sex?

_____

How would you like me to dress for bed?

_____

Day 1

TODAY FIND SOMETHING TO WORK ON TOGETHER. *TEAMWORK* MAKES THE *DREAM* WORK!

Instead of working as individuals today tackle something together. After dinner wash the dishes together, wash-dry-fold clothes together, cook breakfast with one another. This time promotes bonding and trust between couples.
Instead of chores let's play a game:

NAME GAME

For each letter of your partner's name, choose a complimentary adjective to describe them.
Key nugget: Highlight things that foster strength that directly contribute to the health of your relationship

B- Beloved by everyone he meets
R- Reassuring, helps to relieve anxiety
E- Eager to show that he hears my concerns and earnest about showing sincerity
N- Noble, high qualities of dignity
T- Talented and Take-charge in leadership and management style.

M- Motivated to try ANYTHING
A- Attractive especially when she smiles
T- Teachable, she feels she can learn from anyone- (whether it is to do or not to do)
T- Tough and can take a lot without giving up
I- Intelligent, well she is a DR.
E- Energetic, she is always on the go

YOUR TURN!

Day 8

TODAY DO AN ATTITUDE CHECK

Attitude can make or break anything when it comes to relationship. I'm usually told, "it's not what you said, it's how you said it, or the expression on my face while saying it."

3 Attitude Adjustments For Your Marriage:

ALL about the EVERYDAY responses.

Everyday problems and our responses to it can cause damage or good that accumulate over time- Choose your response wisely

Cultivate JOY.

Give each other permission to be happy by asking the right questions and then AIM for JOY.

Trade places for the day.

Maybe you need to see what your partner feels when they are with you. Go overboard and act and talk just like them.... Oh God! Help Us

Day 9

TODAY TAKE TIME TO PRAY FOR YOUR SPOUSE.

Dear_____

I pray for _____

_____
_____
_____
_____
_____
_____
_____
_____
_____
_____

After you pray EXPECT transformation not only in and for your spouse, but in and for yourself.

Day 10

TODAY SHOW SOME AFFECTION.

Many times, we forget about the importance of physical touch or just plain eye contact while talking. Affection allows both partners to experience an increased sense of understanding, love, and harmony.

Later, in the evening after a day full of affectionate touches, calls, text, and kisses...

TRY

BLINDFOLDING

This may not be for everyone, because it involves a significant amount of trust. However, if you both are down for it you can take turns with the blindfold and either ask your partner questions you been wanting to ask or do things you had been wanting to do.
We will leave the rest for you to figure out.

Day 11

TODAY GRANT FORGIVENESS. MAKE THIS A DAY OF FREEDOM.

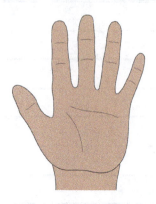

I know, I know you feel like you don't hold grudges. However, sometimes we hold on to toxic hurt or shame which can cause a disconnect we may not have realized from our partner. In order to process negative emotions learning to forgive is imperative for a healthy relationship.

Forgiveness High FIVE

Thumb - "I feel" statements
Index finger - Restate
Middle finger - Ask: Is this correct?
Ring finger - Discuss Solution
Baby finger - Apologize

Day 12

TODAY FIND OUT SOME NEW COMMONALITIES BETWEEN YOU AND YOUR SPOUSE

Finding common interest with your mate is an important ingredient for a successful relationship. Often in the beginning we don't find the importance of having things in common, but the afterglow needs something to help us grow.

1. Do some soul searching. "What brings us joy together?"

2. Ask about their hobbies or what has been interesting to them as of late (*we usually only ask these things in the beginning of our relationship. Things changed*)

3. Plan a date to learn or teach what your mate what you/they love.

_____

_____

_____

_____

Day 13

FIND OUT WHAT MAKES YOUR SPOUSE BEST FRIEND THEIR BEST FRIEND

Being friends does more for the afterglow and the long-term survival of the relationship. Friendships are more important than any other connection we may have. Why? Because usually friends are the family we choose.

If not already.... Ask your mate, "How can I be a part of your inner circle?" The inner circle focuses on understanding, support, and acceptance.

Ask yourself who do I need to be in my mate's inner circle:

- **The Champion** - the cheerleader the one who believes in me
- **The Re-Energizer** - the boost of energy and inspiration person
- **The Connector** - able to introduce you to the right people at the right time
- **Accountability Partner** - your tough love person that will hold you responsible
- **Community Person** - Gives you the sense of belonging and safe space to be yourself
- **Sponsor** - takes charge to advocate for you
- **Mentor** - has greater experience and assist you through wisdom to succeed

Now you just might be a little of all these to your spouse, but they can tell you where they need you the most.

Day 14

CELEBRATE A WIN TODAY

There are always conversations about the trials in relationship and the major point of this book is to catch the positive aspects of one another. Although how we respond in difficult moments is monumental to our relationships rejoicing over each other's accomplishments is a big deal whether big or small.

- Today buy a small gift
- Create an anniversary for this accomplishment
- Unplug from everything else immediately
- Treat each other with a self-care day
- Create a celebratory mantra
- Make them a certificate reminding them of this moment
- Give them a social media shout out

Day 15

RULES FOR MARRIAGE

Never be angry at the **Same** time.

Never yell at each other unless the **house** is on **FIRE.** If one of you must WIN an argument, let it be the other one.

NEVER *bring up* mistakes from the past.

The whole world can be NEGLECTED but not each other.

SETTLE every argument before going to sleep or stay up **ALL NIGHT**.

Remember that it takes two for LOVE.

Day 16

FIND A WAY TO RELAX WITH YOUR PARTNER TODAY

Relaxation decreases the effects of stress on the mind and body. What are some ways you and your spouse relax together?

_____

_____

_____

_____

10 Ways to Relax with Your Partner

1. Take an exercise class together
2. Take a bubble bath together
3. Go to a comedy club together
4. Plan a game night together
5. Find a first to do with each other
6. Just lay in the bed
7. Binge watch a tv show
8. Take a staycation at a hotel
9. Go out with another couple
10. Give each other a massage

Ask your partner how they enjoy relaxing...

Day 17

TODAY TAKE TIME TO LAUGH

Not sure how true the saying is but, I heard that you can't truly love another person if they don't laugh with you or make you laugh. Laughter boosts happy chemicals to the brain. When this is done with your spouse your mind begins to say, "Hey! I'm happy with and around this person."

Here's a few jokes that may make you both laugh

Q. How do all the oceans say hello to each other?
They wave!
Q. What do you call cheese that isn't yours?
Nacho cheese!
Q. What do you call a cow with no legs?
Ground Beef!
Q. Why are ghost such bad liars?
Because you can see right through them!
Q. Why do bees have sticky hair?
They use honeycombs!
Q. Where do cows go for fun?
Moo-vies
Q. What do you call a teethless bear?
A gummy bear!
Q. What do you call a pig that knows karate?
A pork chop!

GET NAKED

Things to do with your mate while naked.

<u>Have a life drawing class</u> - Now of course it doesn't have to be a perfect picture. However, one of you must find a comfortable way to pose while the other person draws you or an interpretation of what they see

<u>Take a shower together</u> - Spend some time washing away the day. Grab a sponge or towel and wipe down your partner's back.

<u>Count each other birth marks or moles</u> - This may sound a little weird but hey! Let's take an adventure while studying our partner's body.

<u>Have SEX</u>
Just do what yawl DO! Have FUNNNN

_____
_____
_____
_____
_____
_____

Day 19

RECOGNIZE HOW YOU MAKE HIM/HER FEEL

"People will forget what you said, people will forget what you did, but people will never forget how you made them feel."

Maya Angelo

How have I made you feel during the time of our relationship, during our time of transition, during the pregnancy (if applies), during the loss of _____?

_____

_____

_____

_____

_____

_____

_____

_____

_____

Day 20

TODAY ASK EACH OTHER, "WHAT AM I MISSING?"

We hope this question foster a closeness that causes mutual vulnerability in the relationship. Allowing yourself to be vulnerable sometimes can be very difficult so hopefully this exercise can help with this issue.

Stare in each other eyes while asking the question— What am I missing?

Write down what they said so you'll never miss it again.

_____

_____

_____

_____

_____

_____

_____

_____

_____

Day 21

MEMORIES

Making memories are essential for mental health. Our purpose and our sense of identity in relationships are built through memories.

Create a memory to strengthen where you are...

Remember a memory to rekindle where you been...

Let's see how well you remember these things or just keep them in mind for next time.

- Where was our first kiss?
- Who said I love you first?
- What did I have on when we met?
- How did we meet?
- What is my favorite color?
- When was the last time I cried?
- What is my favorite food?
- What is my favorite hobby?
- Who do you feel is my go-to person besides you?

_____

_____

_____

_____

Day 22

TODAY JUST DREAM WITH YOUR MATE

When you dream together you strengthen your bond and give each other a visual for the future. Dream for a love, trust, and passion for now and the future.

D - Don't do anything small go BIG
A - Always trust your instinct
R - Resist doubt at all costs
E - Embrace your hearts desire

T - Take charge
O - Overcome procrastination

D - Do it
R - Raise your expectations
E - Expect the best
A - Ask for help/support
M - Manifest

_____
_____
_____
_____
_____
_____

Day 23

TODAY DECIDE TO TRUST YOUR SPOUSE ON ANOTHER LEVEL

One of the greatest and strongest cornerstones of any relationship is trust.

Let's play a game that last forever!

Make your actions match your words.

Consistency is the most important part of trust. Becoming reliable and honest is the best way to create a bond of trust. Remember that trust cannot be built in a day—this is a trust exercise that you can commit to for your full relationship.

A good way to build this trust is to set a date night and always show up on time. This shows your partner that you are committed, consistent and reliable.

_____

_____

_____

_____

_____

_____

_____

_____

Day 24

EXPECT WITH RESPECT

Our deepest wants and needs are reflections that are clouded in expectations.

What are some unspoken expectations you would like to share?

_____
_____
_____
_____
_____
_____
_____
_____
_____
_____
_____
_____

Day 25

TODAY CREATE A BUCKET LIST TOGETHER

1._____

2._____

3._____

4._____

5._____

6._____

7._____

Create this list to reflect what matters most to both of you, your personal values, and to identify important life milestones and experiences that you both want to have.

Make this list as a

SIGN

of Hope

Day 26

TODAY PUSH THE BOUNDARIES OF EACH OTHER'S COMFORT ZONE

"Life begins at the end of your comfort zone."

Often our comfort zone places us in a bubble that could be a hinderance for us reaching new heights. Although leaving your comfort zone can be very stressful doing it together should help to minimize the stress.

What boundary are you looking forward to pushing with your mate?

_____

_____

_____

_____

_____

_____

_____

_____

_____

Day 27

TODAY UNDERSTAND YOU GOT THE BETTER DEAL.

> "A great marriage is one where each partner secretly suspects they got the better deal."

–Unknown

_____
_____
_____
_____
_____
_____
_____
_____

Day 28

TODAY ENJOY YOUR PARTNER'S DIFFERENCE

A great marriage is not when the "perfect couple" comes together. It is when an IMPERFECT couple learns to enjoy their differences.

–Dave Meurer

Day 29

TODAY TRAVEL TO A PLACE UNKNOWN

Share with your mate something that was painfully embarrassing or share something you never shared before.

Day 30

ON THE HUNT

Game Time!!!!

Romantic Scavenger Hunt

Remember playing Treasure Hunt? Why not play it in a romantic way. Design a hunt and leave some cute notes to guide your significant other towards the amazing treat you have planned in advance for them. The gift can be anything from a watch they had been pining for to a romantic candlelight dinner – or YOU!

_____
_____
_____
_____
_____
_____
_____
_____

Day 31

NEVER GIVE UP

Lifelong love does exist, but it also takes work. It is a commitment.

> You can't just give up on someone because the situation's not ideal. Great relationships aren't great because they have no problems. They're great because both people care enough about the other person to find a way to make it work.

CPSIA information can be obtained
at www.ICGtesting.com
Printed in the USA
JSHW030238210222
23105JS00003B/10